W9-CAD-098

EXPLORING WORLD CULTURES

Iran

Joanne Mattern

Cavendish
Square

New York

Published in 2018 by Cavendish Square Publishing, LLC
243 5th Avenue, Suite 136, New York, NY 10016

First Edition

Website: cavendishsq.com

This publication represents the opinions and views of the author based on his or her personal experience, knowledge, and research. The information in this book serves as a general guide only. The author and publisher have used their best efforts in preparing this book and disclaim liability rising directly or indirectly from the use and application of this book.

CPSIA Compliance Information: Batch #CS17CSQ

All websites were available and accurate when this book was sent to press.

Library of Congress Cataloging-in-Publication Data

Names: Mattern, Joanne, 1963- author.
Title: Iran / Joanne Mattern.
Other titles: Exploring world cultures.
Description: New York : Cavendish Square Publishing, 2018. |
Series: Exploring world cultures
Identifiers: LCCN 2016046848 (print) | LCCN 2016056572 (ebook) |
ISBN 9781502624925 (pbk.) | ISBN 9781502624932 (6 pack) |
ISBN 9781502624949 (library bound) | ISBN 9781502624956 (E-book)
Subjects: LCSH: Iran--Juvenile literature.
Classification: LCC DS254.75 .M38 2018 (print) | LCC DS254.75 (ebook) |
DDC 955--dc23
LC record available at https://lccn.loc.gov/2016046848

Editorial Director: David McNamara
Editor: Kristen Susienka
Copy Editor: Rebecca Rohan
Associate Art Director: Amy Greenan
Designer: Joseph Macri
Production Coordinator: Karol Szymczuk
Photo Research: J8 Media

The photographs in this book are used by permission and through the courtesy of: Cover Jason Edwards/National Geographic/Getty Images; p. 5 Matyas Rehak/Shutterstock.com; p. 6 Peter Hermes Furian/Shutterstock.com; p. 7 Marcin Szymczak/Shutterstock.com; p. 8 Borna_Mirahmadian/Shutterstock.com; p. 9 Hulton Archive/Getty Images; p. 10 Chesnot/Getty Images; p. 11 Danita Delimont/Gallo Images/Getty Images; p. 12 anekoho/Shutterstock.com; p. 13 OKcamera/Shutterstock.com; p. 14 fotosaga/Shutterstock.com; p. 15 Tigger11th/Shutterstock.com; p. 16 Hamed Yeganeh/Shutterstock.com; p. 18 Anthony Asael/Art in All of Us/Corbis News/Getty Images; p. 19 Kami/arabianEye/Getty Images; p. 20 Vladimir Melnik/Shutterstock.com; p. 21 Mansoreh/Shutterstock.com; p. 22 imeduard/Shutterstock.com; p. 24 Dmitry Kalinovsky/Shutterstock.com; p. 26 ATTA KENARE/AFP/Getty Images; p. 28 ATTA KENARE/AFP/Getty Images.

Printed in the United States of America

Contents

Introduction

Iran is a country in the Middle East. It is on the continent of Asia. Iran is the second-largest country in the Middle East. Part of Iran is surrounded by land. Other parts are bordered by water. Tehran is the capital of Iran.

Iran has many different landscapes. Part of the land has high mountains. Other parts are covered by desert. The land along the coast is wet and **fertile**.

Almost seventy-nine million people live in Iran. Many different **ethnic** groups make up the country. Iranians speak many different languages. They live in the country and in cities.

Iran has a long and interesting history. The people who live there enjoy sports and games.

They celebrate holidays and share good times with family and friends. Iran is a fascinating nation with many interesting places and cultures.

There are many different goods available for shoppers in an Iranian bazaar.

Iran covers 636,400 square miles (1,648,000 square kilometers). Afghanistan and Pakistan border Iran on the east. Turkey and Iraq border Iran on the west. Azerbaijan, Armenia, and Turkmenistan, and the Caspian Sea lie to the north. The south of Iran borders the Persian Gulf and the Gulf of Oman.

This map shows Iran's location and major cities.

FACT!

The Caspian Sea is not a sea at all. It is really a saltwater lake.

Much of Iran is covered by desert. The Dasht-e Kavir desert is made of salt. Another desert, the Dasht-e Lut, has large sand dunes.

Iran's tallest mountain is Mount Damavand. It is 18,806 feet (5.7 kilometers) tall and is part of the Alborz Mountains. There are many fertile valleys in the Alborz Mountains. The Zagros Mountains lie on Iran's western border.

Whew, It's Hot!

Dasht-e Lut has been called the hottest place on Earth. The temperature can rise as high as 159 degrees Fahrenheit (70.5 degrees Celsius).

The Daht-e Lut desert is beautiful but very harsh.

Iran was once called Persia. People have lived here for tens of thousands of years. By 465 BCE, the Persian **Empire** ruled over all of the Middle East. The empire was finally

Ancient ruins of the Palace of Darius

defeated by Alexander the Great in 330 BCE.

After Alexander died, other dynasties ruled Iran. In 637 CE, Iran became part of the Arab Muslim empire. The country **converted** to a religion called Islam.

Later, Iran became more exposed to Western culture. In 1926, Shah Reza Khan founded the

The Shah Comes and Goes

Shah Muhammad Reza Pahlavi was overthrown twice during his reign: once in 1953 and again in 1979.

Shah Reza Pahlavi and his wife, Soraya, in 1958

Pahlavi Dynasty. This dynasty ruled until 1979. By then, many Iranians wanted to return to traditional Islamic values. They **deposed** the shah. A man named Ayatollah Khomeini ruled Iran as an Islamic republic. It remains one today.

The Persian Empire started with a leader named Kurash, or Cyrus.

Government

Iran has an Islamic government. It was put in place by Ayatollah Khomeini. It puts the rules of God, who is called Allah in Islam, first and the rules of the people second. Iran adopted its **constitution**, or document of laws, in 1979.

Iran's president, Hassan Rouhani, in 2016

Iran's supreme leader is called the *vali-ye faqih*. He is elected by a government assembly and rules for life. He has more power than anyone else.

The Capital City

Tehran is the capital of Iran. It has been the capital since 1795.

The National Garden building in Tehran

Iran's government also has an executive branch. This branch includes the president and the Council of Ministers. The president is elected to a four-year term.

The Islamic Consultative Assembly makes sure that Iran follows Islamic law. Iran's government also includes a Supreme Court and many lower courts.

FACT!

Iran is divided into twenty-eight sections, called provinces. Each province is divided into counties and districts.

11

The Economy

OIL

More than 125 billion barrels of oil lie underneath Iran's land. For many years, Iran shipped oil to countries around the world. However, in 2003, many nations around the world refused to buy Iran's oil. Iran's oil production dropped. The

An oil refinery in Iran. Oil has long been the nation's most important industry.

country turned to other industries, including mining and making machinery, cars, and tractors.

Agriculture is also an important part of Iran's economy. Iran's major crops include sugar, beets, cotton, wool, wheat, rice, and pistachio nuts.

Iran's Money

Iran's money is called the rial. Rials are colorful and include pictures of religious and political figures, as well as important places in Iran.

An Iranian rial features Ayatollah Khomeini.

Iran's people also make beautiful crafts. Weaving Persian carpets is an ancient and popular art. Iranians also produce pottery, leather, silk clothes, and jewelry.

FACT!

Only about 10 percent of Iran's land is good for growing crops. Most of the fertile land is near the Caspian Sea.

About 10 percent of Iran is covered with forests. Ash, elm, and beech trees grow in the Alborz Mountains. Oak, walnut, pear, and pistachio trees grow in the Zagros Mountains.

An oasis, like this one in Iran, provides a green and wet place in the middle of the desert.

Salt cedars, mulberry, plum, and acacia trees grow in desert **oases**. Date palms also grow in many desert areas. Mangrove trees grow in the wet areas along Iran's southern coast.

Iran's largest mammals include ibex, wild sheep, several kinds of deer, leopards, wolves, and jackals. Small animals like rabbits, hares, and ground squirrels also live in the forests. Iran is home to many birds too. Storks and pelicans live along the coast. Owls and eagles live in the forests.

Endangered Animals

Several of Iran's animals are endangered. The government is trying to save Asiatic cheetahs, black bears, and Caspian seals.

The Asiatic black bear is an endangered species.

Air and water pollution are a big problem and threaten Iran's environment.

The People Today

About seventy-eight million people live in Iran. The population includes several different ethnic groups. The largest group is Persians. They make up more than half of the population.

A nomadic girl herds sheep in the Iranian countryside.

The Importance of Tribes

Tribes are very important in nomadic and rural communities. A chief rules a tribe. Tribes have customs that help form strong bonds between the members.

Other ethnic groups include Azeris, Armenians, Kurds, and Arabs. Azeris and Kurds make up about 25 percent of the population. Many live in the northwestern mountains and raise animals like sheep and goats. Some are nomads and travel from place to place, while others live in cities or towns. Arabs make up a small part of Iran's population. Most Arabs live in the southern part of the nation.

FACT!

The cave village of Kandovan is a unique home for Azeris. People have been living in these caves for about three thousand years.

Lifestyle

More than half of Iran's population lives in cities. Most city people live in extended families. An extended family can include parents, children, grandparents, aunts, uncles, and cousins.

These Iranian girls enjoy a drawing class.

Other families live in countryside villages. Houses are simple and built close together. A wall often surrounds the villages to protect them from robbers, sandstorms, and windstorms. Here, families live simply and still do much of their work by hand.

Iranian Weddings

Iranian weddings have two parts. First the bride and groom meet at the bride's parents' house for the Aghd ceremony. After the Aghd comes the Jashn-e Aroosi. This is a party that can last for several days.

A traditional wedding celebration in Iran

Iranian children attend school from Saturday morning until midday on Thursday. Iranian law says all children must go to school until they are twelve years old. Many students go to high school. Some go on to a public or private university.

FACT!

Boys and girls go to separate schools.

Religion

Religion is the most important part of Iranian life. Nearly all Iranians are Muslims, or followers of Islam. Eighty-nine percent of Iran's Muslims belong to a group called Shia. Ten percent are Sunni Muslims.

Men gather for traditional Friday prayers in a mosque.

FACT!

Muslims pray at dawn, midday, mid-afternoon, sunset, and nightfall. Many pray in buildings called mosques. Others pray at home.

All Muslims must follow the Five Pillars of Islam: faith, prayer, fasting, charity, and pilgrimage. Other religious groups in Iran include Baha'i, Zoroastrians, Christians, and Jews. These groups together only make up 1 percent of the population.

Women and Islam

Islam teaches that men and women are equal, but Iran's Islamic law does not treat them equally. Women and men do not go to school together or work together. Women do not have the same freedoms or rights as men.

Iranian women pose in front of beautiful Persian carpets.

Language

Persian is the official language of Iran. More than half of Iranians speak it. Children are taught Persian in school. It is the language used in business, in newspapers, and on television.

A sign made of tiles displays both Western and Persian writing.

Persian has been spoken for thousands of years. This language is written in Arabic script, which is different from writing you might be familiar with. In Arabic script, words read from right to left on the page.

FACT!

Persian is called Farsi in the Persian language.

Although Persian is the official language, Iranians speak other languages too. Each ethnic group has its own language or dialect. These languages include Kurdish, Arabic, Azeri Turkish, Lur, and Baluchi.

Beautiful Writing

Some Iranians write in calligraphy. Calligraphy is a beautiful art form that creates artwork out of written words.

The arts are very important in Iran. Persian stories have been enjoyed for centuries. Some Iranian poetry has religious themes. Other poems tell love stories or stories about heroes.

People play a traditional hammered dulcimer using small hammers.

Iranians also weave carpets and create vases and paintings. They play traditional musical instruments, like the sitar and the *santur*, a drum called a *zarb*, and a flute called a *nay*.

FACT!

Western rock music is not allowed in Iran.

Iranians also celebrate many religious festivals. The most important is a holy month called Ramadan. During Ramadan, Muslims do not eat or drink until after the sun sets. At the end of the month, there is a great celebration called Eid al-Fitr.

Happy New Year!

Now Ruz is a New Year's festival. It is celebrated on March 21. Families and friends celebrate for several days. During Now Ruz, it is traditional for Iranians to jump over a fire to bring good luck in the new year.

Fun and Play

People in Iran enjoy many different sports. Horse racing is very popular in the country. So is polo, which is a sport played on horseback. Many people enjoy watching or playing soccer, tennis, and wrestling. Gymnastics is also popular and is taught to children in school.

Iranian men play a game of polo.

Hossein Rezazadeh is a weightlifter. He was the first Iranian to win two Olympic gold medals. In 2002, he was voted the Champion of Champions of Iran.

Iran's cities have many cafés. Iranians enjoy visiting here to drink tea and talk to their friends. Women enjoy shopping at markets called bazaars and entertaining friends at home. Many people also gather in parks to have a picnic or play a game of chess.

Women and Sports

For many years, women were not allowed to take part in sports. Today, women have more opportunities, but they can only play sports in certain places.

Food

Iranians eat a wide variety of delicious foods. The goal of Iranian cooking is to mix sweet, sour, spicy, and salty flavors. A dish might combine meat, such as lamb, chicken, or duck, with nuts, berries, onions, and a spice called cumin.

An Iranian family enjoys delicious food.

FACT!

Iranians do not eat pork because it is forbidden by the Islamic religion.

Kebabs are a popular dish. They are chunks of meat or fish cooked over hot coals on a long wooden stick called a skewer. Kebabs are served with rice or warm flatbread.

Iranians eat many different fruits and vegetables. Dates, melons, plums, apricots, and peaches are popular fruits. Meals also include salads made of cucumbers and tomatoes. Dairy foods, such as yogurt, are also popular.

Breakfast Is Served!

A popular breakfast in Iran includes sweet tea called chai and flatbread spread with butter or jam. Many Iranians also enjoy eggs for breakfast.

Glossary

agriculture   Farming, growing, and selling crops.

constitution   A document that states the laws of a country.

convert   To change.

depose   To force someone out of public office.

empire   A group of countries under a single ruler.

ethnic   Related to people who have a common national or cultural tradition.

fertile   Land that is able to produce crops.

oases   Places in the desert where there is water, plants, and animals.

Find Out More

Books

Habeeb, William Mark. *Iran*. Philadelphia:

Mason Crest, 2016.

Rajendra, Vijeya. *Cultures of the World: Iran*.

New York: Cavendish Square Publishing, 2015.

Websites

Iran Facts for Kids

http://www.atozkidsstuff.com/iran.html

National Geographic Kids: Iran

http://kids.nationalgeographic.com/explore/

countries/iran/#iran-market.jpg

Video

Iran History and Geography for Kids

https://www.youtube.com/watch?v=YL5xxfwYG58

This video includes many facts about Iran's history,

geography, culture, and more.

Index

About the Author

Joanne Mattern is the author of more than 250 books for children. She specializes in writing nonfiction and has explored many different places in her writing. Her favorite topics include history, travel, sports, biography, and animals. Mattern lives in New York State with her husband, four children, and several pets.